RETREAT
GUIDE

TEACHER
AND LORD

A LENTEN RETREAT GUIDE
ON THE LAST SUPPER

FR. JOHN BARTUNEK, LC, STHD

ISBN-10: 1984921339

ISBN-13: 978-1984921338

This booklet is a part of RCSpirituality's *Retreat Guide* service, which includes free online videos and audio tracks available at **RCSpirituality.org**.

INTRODUCTION

Teacher and Lord

RETREAT OVERVIEW

The highlight of the Church's liturgical year is Holy Week, beginning with Palm Sunday, including Holy Thursday and Good Friday, and culminating with the Easter Vigil and the beginning of the Easter Season.

These are our oldest liturgical feasts. Through them, every single year we commemorate and—in a mysterious way—become present at the most momentous events in the entire history of the world: the passion, death, and resurrection of humanity's one Lord and Savior, Jesus Christ.

During the first centuries of Christianity, the forty days leading up to those celebrations also took on a special significance. Those forty days are called Lent, a name taken from the Old English word meaning "spring." The liturgical season of Lent is meant to be a time of spiritual spring-training, so to speak: six weeks during which we pay particular attention to prayer, penance, and works of mercy in order to prepare for Holy Week. The more deeply we live Lent, the more abundantly we will be able to receive the spiritual renewal that God wants to give us during the holiest days of the liturgical year.

This Retreat Guide on the Last Supper, *Teacher and Lord*, will help make that happen.

o   The First Meditation takes us into what was going on in Christ's own heart during his last meal with his closest followers.

o   The Second Meditation highlights the three precious gifts that Jesus left his Church during the Last Supper, and the hopes he had for how those gifts can transform our lives.

o   And the Conference provides practical tips for how we can deepen our friendship with Christ through the words we use.

Let's begin by opening our hearts to the Lord and asking him for all the graces we need, especially the grace to let Jesus be, more and more completely, our Teacher and our Lord.

NOTES

FIRST MEDITATION

Love and Sorrow

INTRODUCTION

St. John the Evangelist's account of the Last Supper reveals the deepest meaning behind Christ's passion, death, and resurrection. Here is what he writes in the very first verse of the thirteenth chapter of his Gospel:

> Before the feast of Passover, Jesus knew that his hour had come to pass from this world to the Father. He loved his own in the world and he loved them to the end.
>
> —John 13:1

Jesus knew that "his hour had come." Throughout John's Gospel, references to Jesus' "hour" appear frequently. It's the term St. John uses to refer to Christ's passion, death, and resurrection—the central events in the redemption of the fallen human race.

AT CHRIST'S CORE

And what is our Lord's motivation to work for that redemption, to accept the suffering that his "hour" would entail? Love. His—God's—love for us broken, sinful human beings. That's the engine, the heart, behind everything Jesus did, and especially behind his obedience up until death on the cross—a loving obedience to his Father that would reverse and atone for the self-centered disobedience of every human sin since the sin of Adam and Eve in the Garden of Eden.

The phrase St. John uses to explain this motivation of love is worth considering more deeply. He says that Jesus, having loved his own in the world—his followers, the people he came to call and redeem—now "loves them to the end." What is St. John getting at here?

GOD'S UNDENIABLY UNCONDITIONAL LOVE

Spiritual writers and biblical scholars have reflected on that phrase since the early years of the Church. Most of them agree about what John is getting at.

Jesus gave many proofs of his love during his years on earth—his companionship with his followers, his miraculous healings, his liberation of so many people from demonic influence, and all his teachings about where true happiness and meaning can be found.

And yet, he knew the human heart well. He knew that because of original sin and all the wounds to our hearts that come from experiencing the brokenness of this fallen world, it is hard for us to truly believe in God's unconditional love. It is hard for us to truly, fully trust that God loves us. Sometimes we think that we have failed and sinned too much. Other times we think that we are simply too inconsequential, too small. Still other times we get stuck in thinking—consciously or unconsciously—that the Christian life is really about *earning* God's love, about working hard to make ourselves worthy of his love.

But those are all distortions of the truth. Yes, we are sinners. Yes, we are small, limited creatures. Yes, we are called to make good use of the gifts we have been given. All of that is true. But none of those truths mean that God is holding back his love, his care, his interest, or his grace. He is not waiting for us to become perfect in order to begin loving us. On the contrary, it is his unconditional and merciful love that actually initiates our whole journey of healing, redemption, and spiritual growth—his love precedes ours; our love is always a response to his.

GOD'S INEXTINGUISHABLE COMMITMENT

Jesus knew that it's hard for us to accept and understand that. So he decided to give us yet another proof of his love, something more radical than his teaching and his miracles. He decided to give us the *supreme* proof of his absolute, infinite, unlimited love. This is what St. John means when he writes that Jesus, "loved those who were his own in the world, and he loved them *to the end*."

Throughout all the spiritual, moral, emotional, and physical pain of his passion—from the Garden of Gethsemane, being abandoned and betrayed by his closest friends, to being unjustly condemned by the Sanhedrin and by Pontius Pilate, through his scourging, humiliation, crowning with thorns, and crucifixion, Jesus was "loving us to the end," to the extreme, showing that no matter what this sinful, fallen world does, nothing can extinguish God's commitment to us, nothing can ever make God the Father abandon his children or give up on them.

JESUS REVEALS THE FATHER

Later during the Last Supper Jesus told his Apostles, "Whoever has seen me has seen the Father" (John 14:9). Jesus accepted the hideous, violent assaults of evil without ever retaliating, without ever condemning his enemies, without ever altering the gaze of goodness and love that had shone without fail from his glorious face since the day of his birth. As St. Peter describes it in his First New Testament Letter:

> When he was insulted, he returned no insult; when he suffered, he did not threaten; instead, he handed himself over to the one who judges justly. He himself bore our sins in his body upon the cross, so that, free from sin, we might live for righteousness.
>
> —1 Peter 2:23–24

And St. Paul puts it even more succinctly:

> But God proves his love for us in that while we were still sinners Christ died for us.
>
> —Romans 5:8

A TROUBLED HEART

So the desire to give a supreme proof of God's unconditional love for each one of us—a proof that would stand the test of time and be strong enough to break down all our suspicions, fears, and doubts—was in Christ's heart as he endured his passion and death. But something else was there too.

St. John describes it like this:

> When he had said this, Jesus was deeply troubled and testified, "Amen, amen, I say to you, one of you will betray me"
>
> —John 13:21

This isn't the first time St. John tells us that Jesus' heart was troubled. In the previous Chapter, when Jesus is speaking about his coming passion, right after his triumphal entry into Jerusalem on Palm Sunday, he says:

> I am troubled now. Yet what should I say? "Father, save me from this hour"? But it was for this purpose that I came to this hour. Father, glorify your name.
>
> —John 12:27–28

Jesus feels anguish in his heart, mind, and soul even before he begins to be tormented in his body. He knows what his Father is asking of him—to redeem the world through suffering, through absorbing all the sin and guilt of the world into his own soul, knowing the indescribable agony it will cause him—and it makes him tremble.

SORROWFUL UNTO DEATH

The other Gospel writers describe just how much Jesus was troubled when they tell us about his prayer later on Holy Thursday, in the Garden of Gethsemane right after the Last Supper:

> He took with him Peter, James, and John, and began to be troubled and distressed. Then he said to them, "My soul is sorrowful even to death. Remain here and keep watch." He advanced a little and fell to the ground and prayed that if it were possible the hour might pass by him ... He was in such agony and he prayed so fervently that his sweat became like drops of blood falling on the ground.
>
> —Mark 14:33–35; Luke 22:44

Love and sorrow, these were the melodies playing in Our Lord's heart throughout his passion. Infinite love for each one of us, which makes almost infinitely intense the sorrow he felt for all the damage that sin has done, is doing, and will do to the human family. Love and sorrow, two of our deepest human experiences, and Jesus makes them his own in a dramatic way throughout his passion.

Love and sorrow are the keys that can unlock all the lessons Jesus wants to teach us, all the graces that he wants to send us, through our Lenten contemplation of his passion, death, and resurrection. In the next meditation, we will look at the three gifts Jesus gave during the Last Supper, but for now, we may want to take some time, in the quiet of our hearts, to enter into that contemplation. The following questions and quotations may help your meditation.

QUESTIONS FOR PERSONAL REFLECTION/GROUP DISCUSSION

1. In his passion, Jesus loved us "to the end." What are my initial reactions when I hear God's love described as limitless and unconditional? Where are those reactions rooted? Speak to our Lord about that.

2. Under what circumstances do I find it hard to trust God? Why? What would Jesus say about that?

3. Jesus experienced sorrow and suffering in this fallen world. How does knowing this redefine my own experience of sorrow and suffering? How does it relate to the ubiquitous Catholic prayer of the Sign of the Cross?

We know that all things work for good for those who love God, who are called according to his purpose … What then shall we say to this? If God is for us, who can be against us? He who did not spare his own Son but handed him over for us all, how will he not also give us everything else along with him? Who will bring a charge against God's chosen ones? It is God who acquits us. Who will condemn? It is Christ [Jesus] who died, rather, was raised, who also is at the right hand of God, who indeed intercedes for us.

—Romans 8:28; 31–34
NABRE

What will separate us from the love of Christ? Will anguish, or distress, or persecution, or famine, or nakedness, or peril, or the sword? … No, in all these things we conquer overwhelmingly through him who loved us. For I am convinced that neither death, nor life, nor angels, nor principalities, nor present things, nor future things, nor powers, nor height, nor depth, nor any other creature will be able to separate us from the love of God in Christ Jesus our Lord.

—Romans 8:35; 37–39
NABRE

The clearest proof of the reliability of Christ's love is to be found in his dying for our sake. If laying down one's life for one's friends is the greatest proof of love (cf. Jn 15:13), Jesus offered his own life for all, even for his enemies, to transform their hearts. This explains why the evangelists could see the hour of Christ's crucifixion as the culmination of the gaze of faith; in that hour the depth and breadth of God's love shone forth. It was then that Saint John offered his solemn testimony, as together with the Mother of Jesus he gazed upon the pierced one (cf. Jn 19:37): "He who saw this has borne witness, so that you also may believe. His testimony is true, and he knows that he tells the truth" (Jn 19:35). In Dostoevsky's *The Idiot*, Prince Myshkin sees a painting by Hans Holbein the Younger depicting Christ dead in the tomb and says: "Looking at that painting might cause one to lose his faith." [14] The painting is a gruesome portrayal of the destructive effects of death on Christ's body. Yet it is precisely in contemplating Jesus' death that faith grows stronger and receives a dazzling light; then it is revealed as faith in Christ's steadfast love for us, a love capable of embracing death to bring us salvation. This love, which did not recoil before death in order to show its depth, is something I can believe in; Christ's total self-gift overcomes every suspicion and enables me to entrust myself to him completely.

—*Lumen Fidei*, 16
POPE FRANCIS

NOTES

SECOND MEDITATION

Three Gifts from the Last Supper

INTRODUCTION

Jesus' first words during the Last Supper, according to the Gospel of Luke, reveal that there's even more in his heart than the love and sorrow we contemplated in the first meditation. Here is what he said:

> When the hour came, he took his place at table with the apostles. He said to them, "I have eagerly desired to eat this Passover with you before I suffer."

—Luke 22:14–15

DESIRING WITH DESIRE

In the original Greek, the two words "eagerly desired" are actually the same word, just used in two different ways—once as a verb, and once as an adverb. The Greek term is "epithymia", and it means deep, burning desire, the type of feeling that springs from the very core of the soul. By using this word twice in a row, the Scriptures are telling us that Christ's whole heart and soul were fully engaged in the drama of the Last Supper.

Some biblical scholars translate it differently in order to try and communicate the intensity of Our Lord's earnestness during those hours. Instead of saying, "I have eagerly desired …" they translate the Greek as meaning "with desire I have desired …" This is a more literal translation, and its very awkwardness in English seems to embody the overflowing, almost inexpressible emotion of this encounter Jesus has with his closest followers.

FULFILLING THE OLD WITH SOMETHING NEW

But why was Jesus so eager for this particular Passover celebration? During the Last Supper, Jesus alters the ancient Jewish Passover ritual, showing clearly that the sacrifice of the Passover lamb that preceded and commemorated Israel's miraculous liberation from slavery in Egypt was an image, a prefiguring of Christ's own self-sacrifice on the Cross that would open the door to liberation from sin and death.

In fact, the whole experience of the Chosen People in the Old Testament was a prefiguring of and a preparation for the New Testament. Christ himself fulfills the promises of the Old Covenant and establishes his New, eternal Covenant through the shedding of his blood on the cross. That Covenant will make everyone who believes in Christ and follows him a true child of God, through grace. As St. John put it at the beginning of his Gospel:

But to all who received him, who believed in his name, he gave power to become children of God; who were born, not of blood nor of the will of the flesh nor of the will of man, but of God.

—John 1:12–13

The Last Supper is intimately connected to that sacrifice, to that New Covenant, through the three gifts that Jesus left us during it. These three gifts enable us to actually participate in Christ's redemption, not just admire it from a distance. These gifts also keep Christ's own life, the life of grace, flowing through his Mystical Body, the Church. Through these gifts Christ's life in us continues to be nourished, renewed, and protected.

Maybe that's why Jesus so eagerly desired to eat this final Passover with his Apostles, because he knew that he would be giving them these gifts, and he simply couldn't wait.

GIVING HIMSELF

The first of the gifts is the Eucharist. It was during the Last Supper, through consecrating bread and wine into his body and blood, that Jesus made a connection between the ancient Passover ritual, the eternal heavenly banquet, and the Celebration of the Eucharist. The Eucharist, through the Mass, links past, present, and future through a sacramental mystery. Here is how St. Matthew records the institution of the Eucharist during the Last Supper:

> Now as they were eating, Jesus took bread, and blessed, and broke it, and gave it to the disciples and said, "Take, eat; this is my body." And he took a cup, and when he had given thanks he gave it to them, saying, "Drink of it, all of you; for this is my blood of the covenant, which is poured out for many for the forgiveness of sins. I tell you I shall not drink again of this fruit of the vine until that day when I drink it new with you in my Father's kingdom"

—Matthew 26:26–29

Just as the ancient Israelites ate the flesh of the Passover lamb and put its blood on their doors when God established the Old Covenant and liberated them from earthly slavery, so too every one of us is called to partake of the body and blood of God's true sacrificial lamb, Christ, through receiving the Eucharist. And every time we participate in Mass and receive Holy Communion worthily, we extend the redeeming work of Christ more fully into our lives and into the world around us. His work of salvation was accomplished once and for all on Calvary, when he repaired the ancient breach between heaven and earth. But through us, through our sacramental union with him in the Eucharist, that work continues to spread into every corner of time and space.

This is why Blessed Pope Paul VI could write that the celebration of the Eucharist is the source and summit of the life of the Church and the focal point of all the Church's efforts at evangelization:

> To live the sacraments in this way, bringing their celebration to a true fullness, is not, as some would claim, to impede or to accept a distortion of evangelization: it is rather to complete it. For in its totality, evangelization—over and above the preaching of a message—consists in the implantation of the Church, which does not exist without the driving force which is the sacramental life culminating in the Eucharist.
>
> —*Evangelii Nuntiandi*, 28

BUILDING AN INDESTRUCTIBLE BRIDGE

The second gift that Jesus gave us during the Last Supper was another sacramental gift, the sacrament of Holy Orders.

After Jesus consecrated the bread and wine into his sacred body and blood, anticipating his sacrifice on the cross, he commanded his Apostles: "Do this in remembrance of me" (Luke 22:19). With those words, Jesus empowered his Apostles to celebrate the Eucharist and to ordain others to do the same. He desired to link the celebration of the New Testament sacraments to an order of New Testament priests, similar to how God had linked Old Testament worship to the Levitical priesthood.

Through the presence of ordained clergy, the Church in every corner of the world, throughout every period of history, is given by Christ an objective, sacramental connection to the Last Supper, the Crucifixion, and the Resurrection. The unbroken chain of bishops and priests spread across the centuries enables each one of us to participate in the same sacraments and receive the same redeeming grace that the Apostles themselves received directly from Christ. It is a guarantee of authenticity given to every generation of Christians.

PARTNERS IN BUILDING UP THE KINGDOM

The third gift Jesus gave us at the Last Supper was his New Commandment. He promised that if we keep his commands we will maintain a union with him that is as close as the union between a vine and its branches. Then he described how all his commands are summed up in one New Commandment:

This is my commandment: love one another as I love you. No one has greater love than this, to lay down one's life for one's friends. You are my friends if you do what I command you.

—John 15:12–14

Jesus allows his own divine life—his redeeming grace—to enter and transform our lives, through the Eucharist and all the other sacraments. But then he invites and enables us to become partners in making that grace fruitful by choosing to love as he loves. Grace isn't like magic. Grace is real participation in the life of Christ, but its fruit in our souls and in the world around us depends on our free cooperation, on our decision to love as Christ loves in our everyday lives.

WASHING EACH OTHER'S FEET

Only in this context does the unforgettable Last Supper gesture of Jesus washing his disciples' feet, which we commemorate liturgically every Holy Thursday, take on its fullest meaning.

We are called to build up Christ's Kingdom in ourselves and in the world through following the example of Jesus, who humbled himself, serving his disciples by performing a lowly, inglorious task reserved to slaves. Here is how Jesus himself explained it to his stunned Apostles after he had finished washing their feet:

When he had washed their feet, and taken his garments, and resumed his place, he said to them, "Do you know what I have done to you? You call me Teacher and Lord; and you are right, for so I am. If I then, your Lord and Teacher, have washed your feet, you also ought to wash one another's feet. For I have given you an example, that you also should do as I have done to you. Truly, truly, I say to you, a servant is not greater than his master; nor is he who is sent greater than he who sent him. If you know these things, blessed are you if you do them."

—John 13:12–17

The gift of Holy Orders, to keep grace flowing into the Church and the world for all time; the gift of the Eucharist, to be supernatural nourishment along our pilgrimage of faith; and the gift of the New Commandment, a light to guide our every action and decision as we strive day by day to learn from Christ our Teacher and to obey Christ our Lord. Such great and wonderful gifts—no wonder Jesus "desired with desire" to eat that meal with his Apostles.

In the Conference, we will reflect on one concrete way we can live out that New Commandment. But for now, let's take some time to reflect prayerfully on the meaning of these gifts, and on what use we are making of them. The following questions and quotations may help your meditation.

QUESTIONS FOR PERSONAL REFLECTION/GROUP DISCUSSION

1. What would "washing one another's feet" look like in my life? Where do I find it hard to serve others in my daily life? Speak with Our Lord about those relationships and situations.

2. How much do I appreciate the amazing continuity of the Church throughout history provided for by the sacrament of Holy Orders? How firmly do I believe that Jesus has chosen to touch my life with his grace

in an objective way through the sacramental ministry of his priests? How does that make me feel?

3. What role does the Eucharist play in my life? What role would I like it to play? What can I do to make this gift of our Lord more fruitful for my heart, mind, and soul?

QUOTATIONS TO HELP YOUR PRAYER

*When he [Judas] had left, Jesus said, "Now is the Son of Man glorified, and God is glorified in him. [If God is glorified in him,] God will also glorify him in himself, and he will glorify him at once. My children, I will be with you only a little while longer. You will look for me, and as I told the Jews, 'Where I go you cannot come,' so now I say it to you. I give you a new commandment: love one another. As I have loved you, so you also should love one another. This is how all will know that you are my disciples, if you have love for one another."

—John 13:31–35
NABRE

*Before the feast of Passover, Jesus knew that his hour had come to pass from this world to the Father. He loved his own in the world and he loved them to the end. The devil had already induced Judas, son of Simon the Iscariot, to hand him over. So, during supper, fully aware that the Father had put everything into his power and that he had come from God and was returning to God, he rose from supper and took off his outer garments. He took a towel and tied it around his waist. Then he poured water into a basin and began to wash the disciples' feet and dry them with the towel around his waist … So when he had washed their feet [and] put his garments back on and reclined at table again, he said to them, "Do you realize what I have done for you? You call me 'teacher' and 'master,' and rightly so, for indeed I am. If I, therefore, the master and teacher, have washed your feet, you ought to wash one another's feet. I have given you a model to follow, so that as I have done for you, you should also do."

—John 13:1–5; 12–15
NABRE

When the hour came, he took his place at table with the apostles. He said to them, "I have eagerly desired to eat this Passover with you before I suffer, for, I tell you, I shall not eat it [again] until there is fulfillment in the kingdom of God." Then he took a cup, gave thanks, and said, "Take this and share it among yourselves; for I tell you [that] from this time on I shall not drink of the fruit of the vine until the kingdom of God comes." Then he took the bread, said the blessing, broke it, and gave it to them, saying, "This is my body, which will be given for you; do this in memory of me." And likewise the cup after they had eaten, saying, "This cup is the new covenant in my blood, which will be shed for you."

—Luke 22:14–20
NABRE

NOTES

CONFERENCE

Christlike Love in Our Words

INTRODUCTION

"Love one another as I have loved you" (John 15:12). That is Christ's New Commandment, his Last Supper gift to the Church, to all of us, that allows us to become co-redeemers with him, to be his partners in the extension of his Kingdom to every corner of our own lives, and to every corner of this beautiful, fallen world. With his grace at work in us, our choices to love as Christ loved truly can be the catalyst for growth in holiness, happiness, and supernatural fruitfulness day by day.

Many of the ways we express this love—the works of mercy, as Catholic spirituality traditionally calls them—are not available to us every single day. We can bury the dead and visit the sick only occasionally, for example. But there is something that all of us do every day that, if we want, can become a constant expression of Christlike love: talk.

We talk every day, all the time. We talk with our voices, and we also talk with the words we put in our text messages, emails, and social media interventions. We are constantly communicating with words. But how often do we recognize in this flow of talk a chance to love like Christ? This Conference is an attempt to help us recognize it, and take advantage of it, all the time.

THE POWER OF THE TONGUE

In the New Testament Letter of St. James, the Scriptures dramatically highlight speech, human communication, as a privileged sphere of Christian activity and virtue. In James, Chapter 3, we read:

❝ … [W]e all fall short in many respects. If anyone does not fall short in speech, he is a perfect man, able to bridle his whole body also. If we put bits into the mouths of horses to make them obey us, we also guide their whole bodies. It is the same with ships: even though they are so large and driven by fierce winds, they are steered by a very small rudder wherever the pilot's inclination wishes. In the same way the tongue is a small member and yet has great pretensions.

—James 3:2–5

These are vivid images about how the power of our words—the tongue, in St. James's vocabulary—can influence our lives and the lives of those around us. But he doesn't stop there. In the next few verses, he continues with even more vivid and attention-grabbing comparisons. He writes:

❝ Consider how small a fire can set a huge forest ablaze. The tongue is also a fire. It exists among our members as a world of malice, defiling the whole body and setting the entire course of our lives on fire, itself set on fire by Gehenna. For every kind of beast and bird, of reptile and sea creature, can be tamed and has been tamed by the human species, but no human being can tame the tongue. It is a restless evil, full of deadly poison. With it we bless the Lord and Father, and with it we curse human beings who are made in the likeness of God. From the same mouth come blessing and cursing. This need not be so, my brothers.

—James 3:2–10

Malicious words can cause so much damage, and our fallen human nature gives us all a strong tendency to use words destructively. And yet, St. James ends by saying, "This need not be so, my brothers."

GRACIOUS WORDS: SWEETNESS TO THE SOUL

If human speech has powerful potential for evil, it must also have powerful potential for good. Our experience proves that this is the case. Just remember how many times the right word of advice, encouragement, mercy, or compassion has relieved a seemingly unbearable burden of stress, confusion, or disappointment. In a real sense, words have the power to give new life, to resurrect a soul stuck in the tomb of sadness, ignorance, or hopelessness. Words can do this. Words are powerful. The Book of Proverbs puts it like this:

Gracious words are like a honeycomb,
   sweetness to the soul and health to the body.

—Proverbs 16:24

FROM THE FULLNESS OF THE HEART

Think about the seven spiritual works of mercy; they all happen through words, through communication: counseling the doubtful, comforting the afflicted, admonishing the sinner, forgiving injuries, instructing the ignorant, praying for the living and the dead—even bearing wrongs patiently manifests itself through words, through resisting the temptation to lash out at someone who has wronged us with hurtful, vengeful speech.

Words contain this power because words are linked to our spiritual core, to our heart. Language is something particularly human, connected to our being created in the image of God and called to communion with God through our friendship with Christ, who is the Word of God. Jesus pointed out this deeply spiritual and human significance of our words when he said, "For from the fullness of the heart the mouth speaks" (Matthew 12:34).

Every time we speak, every time we tweet or text, we have a chance to reflect outwardly the grace, truth, and Christlike love dwelling in our hearts. And every time we do that, we build up the everlasting Kingdom of Christ.

SINS OF SPEECH

To help us take full advantage of these opportunities, and to help us experience the fulfillment that comes from loving as Christ loves, whether in deed, thought, or word, it will be useful to review the pitfalls to avoid, and the targets to shoot for, in our words. This is especially important because today's "post-truth" culture of constant digital communication seems to have completely forgotten about even basic moral decency in this area.

LYING

The most obvious sin in our words is lying. If we aren't speaking and communicating the truth, without exaggeration or falsification, we are misusing the great gift of speech. By words, we are meant to build communion with others, connect with others, and foster authentic relationships and mutual understanding. Lies do just the opposite. And the funny thing is, whenever we lie once, we soon find ourselves having to keep on lying in order to keep the deception going. Lying, like all sins, spreads like an infection.

CALUMNY AND SLANDER

When we spread lies about other people, the gravity of the sin increases. This type of lying is called calumny or slander. Spiritual writers through the ages have compared calumny to a kind of verbal murder. With our false words we destroy other people's reputations and make it impossible for them to live normal, fruitful lives. We can do irreparable damage with calumny, which is why repenting from this sin always requires us to make an attempt to repair whatever damage we caused.

DETRACTION AND GOSSIP

We can also do damage to other people even when we speak truthfully about them. We can talk to others about their faults and failures, for example, when there is absolutely no need to do so. We can spread stories about their mistakes and their flaws, stories that may be true, but that other people have no right to know, and that will change forever the way they see that person. This sin is called detraction, and it is common fodder for gossip and tale bearing. This is an abusive use of the truth, and we should avoid it like the plague that it is—we should avoid doing it, and we should also stop it or refuse to listen when other people do it.

Whenever we are speaking about other people, our basic rule of thumb should be to avoid saying or listening to anything that we wouldn't say if that person were in the room with us. That's a concrete application of our Lord's golden rule: "Love your neighbor as yourself" (Mark 12:31).

ASSORTED PITFALLS

Flattery and boasting are other ways that we can deviate from the truth and use words to distort relationships instead of building authentic communion.

And harsh, wounding, or destructive criticism is another way to abuse the truth; it is often the result of uncontrolled anger. When we see something that can be improved, we should choose the circumstances and manner of speaking about it that will build others up, not tear them down. This is what constructive criticism, loving and wise feedback, is all about.

If we tend to keep falling into one of these sins on a regular basis, it would be worthwhile to reflect deeply on why. There could be some fear or self-protection mechanism at the root of the habit, something that needs to be touched by God's grace, healed, and removed from the garden of our soul.

CONCLUSION: BUILDING CHRIST'S KINGDOM THROUGH HOW WE SPEAK

Those are the destructive ways of using words that we should avoid. But what about the positive use of words? We have already reviewed the seven works of spiritual mercy, which open up a wide arena for loving others with Christlike love through what we say. But I would like to finish this conference with a quotation from St. Paul, who gives a good summary of what we should strive for, as Christians, in our speech and communication. In his Letter to the Ephesians he writes:

   Do not use harmful words in talking. Use only helpful words, the kind that build up and provide what is needed, so that what you say will do good to those who hear you. And do not make God's Holy Spirit sad; for the Spirit is God's mark of ownership on you, a guarantee that the Day will come when God will set you free. Get rid of all bitterness, passion, and anger. No more shouting or insults. No more hateful feelings of any sort. Instead, be kind and tender-hearted to one another, and forgive one another, as God has forgiven you in Christ.

—Ephesians 4:29–32[1]

Let's welcome the gift of Christ's new commandment, the gift he gave us at the Last Supper so that we can actively cooperate with the flourishing of God's saving grace in our lives and in our world. And let's start with the handiest tools at our disposal—our words.

The following questionnaire will help you apply these general spiritual truths to your particular life situation.

---

[1]   Translation from *The Divine Office* version approved by the hierarchies of Australia, England and Wales, and Ireland.

PERSONAL QUESTIONNAIRE

1. How often have I reflected on the power of words? How convinced am I that my words really are a daily arena where I can contribute to or hinder the building up of Christ's Kingdom?

2. How firmly do I desire to love my neighbor as myself with my words? How firmly does Jesus desire it?

3. What role, if any, does lying play in my life?

4. What role, if any, does calumny play in my life?

5. What role, if any, does detraction, gossip, and tale-bearing play in my life?

6. What role, if any, do flattery, boasting, and destructive criticism play in my life?

7. In what situations do I tend to say things that I later regret? What can I do to avoid falling into that behavior in the future?

8. What role does silence play in my life? In light of that question, reflect on this passage: "He who restrains his words has knowledge, and he who has a cool spirit is a man of understanding. Even a fool, when he keeps silent, is considered wise; when he closes his lips, he is considered prudent" (Proverbs 17:27–28).

9. How good of a listener would I consider myself? How good of a listener would my family members consider me? My colleagues? What could I do this week to be a better listener?

10. Review the spiritual works of mercy. [Comforting the afflicted, counseling the doubtful, instructing the ignorant, admonishing the sinner, forgiving injuries, bearing wrongs patiently, praying for the living and the dead]. Which of them do I have frequent opportunities to engage in? What can I do to take better advantage of those opportunities?

NOTES

FURTHER READING

If you feel moved to continue reflecting and praying about this theme, you may find the following books helpful:

The Passion and Death of Our Lord Jesus Christ
by Alban Goodier, SJ

*The Better Part: A Christ-Centered
Resource for Personal Prayer*
by Fr. John Bartunek, LC

Inside the Passion
by Fr. John Bartunek, LC

*Sharpening Your Tongue: A Regnum Christi
Essay on Charity in Our Words*
by Fr. John Bartunek, LC

The Catechism of the Catholic Church
Numbers 2464–2513

EXPLORING MORE

Please visit our website, *RCSpirituality.org*, for more spiritual resources, and follow us on Facebook for regular updates: *facebook.com/RCSpirituality*.

If you would like to support and sponsor a Retreat Guide, please consider making a donation at RCSpirituality.org.

Retreat Guides are a service of Regnum Christi. *RegnumChristi.org*

Produced by Coronation Media. *CoronationMedia.com*

Developed & Self-published by RCSpirituality. *RCSpirituality.org*